i am the poet of desire

i am the poet of desire

desire

JOHN OAKLEY MCELHENNEY

Press of Light and Space ● Austin, Texas

i've set myself on

fire

for you i've set myself on fire
a hundred times
checking your emergency
responses

disappointments
continue
as my fever reaches dangerous heights
thoughts blurring
trajectory inverting back toward
blackness
thick
dark
loneliness
a story i learned as a boy
by the lake

knowing when to stop
give up
leave

and when to try again
optimistic
still starving in the silence
between kisses

she was right
there was no way
in
her heart was full and still filling
in her self-described
chaos beautiful
soccer tennis math reading bedtime routines
of single motherhood
and sons

but the fierce independence
that captured my imagination
a strong woman
was misguided and misconstrued
her constant vigilance
against all threats
forever
and
ever

it was her and her child
tangled in her unruly hair

where i hoped to find some purchase
each night
she returned to the big bed
smelling of Ironman shampoo

"i'm beat"
a telegraphed message
we can snuggle for a bit
then you've got to go
it was how she needed it to be
sleeping alone in a kingsized bed
in case
of
intruders

tasting snow

the images dreams plans

are never happening

a frigid chill swept over all of us

one of us

me

is fighting to relight the fire

one of us

you

building excel formulas anticipating child support

good morning love

i am here
cannot feel you
or see
reaching out
there is a beautiful view
without wifi

coffee cold

sending vibes
across our secret network
trust
hope
kisses still warming my heart

the gun was

loaded, safety off

if a gun appears
it is bound to go off
where you will be
is the jam
in the path of the bullet
or in a different state
room
time

inspired by hunter s thompson

the end of poetry

it was a great run
these letters
words
not sentences
all arranged to make sounds
in your mind

when the last poetry shop closed
i was saddened beyond comprehension
less for me
more for the kids
who cannot know the value
of the letter "i"
the passion of the unpunctuated line break
the drift of language and sound
blending together
into something
irrelevant
yet irreplaceable

if the poet has been hung out to dry
and all we have left is tiktok dances
and viral videos of jackass stunts
i think i'll call it a night
either i'm poet laureate by summer
or i'm gone
ffs

i
not at a loss for words
but
sounds no longer
have a place to vibrate
with an appreciative audience
a pause
whisper
snort and chuckle
sweet prince
dead
done
da da

i'm about half as

tired

i am down but I was up just a little bit awhile a go
feelin high singin songs smiling through the light in the hotel
room window
but now I'm done, can't find what's on the ground on in my
mind
i'm underneath in between i'll be right back with who I really
wanted to be tonight

if you'll excuse me please, it won't take but a day or two or a
week
sometimes when I hit it just right i could be back here in an
hour swimming in the pool

but nothing is cool about this foolishness today
nothing's colder than the grip of icy fingers across the back of
my neck
i won't be down for long, cause i don't play this way

but when I can, I let the time and the rest and the gaming lead
the way

just wanna be with me wanna be talky or play a game.
ya wanna go fishing go somewhere different we can have
coffee in a new cafe
every day don't ya think

cause there's nothing to be done for it that ain't already be done
there ain't no vibe that a kicking rock song can't find an edge
something so pretty something of sparkling bliss
that can pick me up take me out of this state

i'm about half as tired as when i went to sleep last night
all the words and projects and figuring it out
never gave my gentle thoughts equal time
i've been like this before and if I can move beyond the bum
i can sometimes find my way into fascination

fascination and creativity are doors out of this hole i'm in
singing connects all of my arts with word soul resonance
breath...
performing for people sets me free
shows all of my parts

not all the same

slow motion pain
we are not all the same
losses
tear some of us deeper
loves lost
wound us
at depths we will never fathom
she was here
she was gone
she is never coming back
yet
she never leaves

spitting fire

there she was in her little black dress
just crossing the bridge towards me
spitting fire
asking me to engage
or be enflamed to bursting

time to go

i didn't really pack my stuff when i left
i wasn't in a clear space
it was the end of the world
as i imagined it
two kids
dog and cat
lovely and unhappy wife
coming apart
with a single word
attorney

nothing would ever mean as much to me
i was unable to imagine
survival
no books or bed

as i burst into sad smoldering ruins
my now-ex
packed my entire universe

in boxes bound for the garage
with her best friend
and friend of mine since 4th grade
i was spared the heartache
politely rooted out
deleted from my former abode
and the young lives
no longer believing
i would tuck them in
or wake them for my famous french toast
before the bus

a little bit about

energy

what if i told you
well actually i'm just making this shit up
but... if i told you
that the fountain of youth is energy
and how you manage yours
each and every day
that a second cup of coffee
placed strategically
between lunch and bedtime
might impart superpowers
powers of insight
inspiration
poetry

yep

right here

this word
this carriage return
these letters without pauses
were given to me
care of my afternoon cuppa

besides that
i picked up almost two hours today
by *not* needing a nap
this work from home stuff
it's so taxing

okay, let's review
drink coffee
twice

let's see where you go from there

years of falling

all these seasons past
fire smoke in the air
and loss and loneliness
prayers longing and loss
have framed the years
the morning air
aching for snuggles and blankets
of hopeful partners
passed by and released

this bright morning
has a new shine
her name is YES
her name is ALWAYS
her name is AVAILABLE

intention and best wishes
can build a partnership
but only complete surrender

burns away the old hurts
scorches darkness into carbon dust
releasing us to bind
mend and rebuild each touchpoint
leading towards a hand
to hold forever
and breathless affirmations
while together
remain after she has gone
this morning is a rebirth
a new hope
a homecoming
in a blur of kisses
spinning higher towards the sky of stars
above us
together

letting me go

she seems to have had little problem letting me go
falling away
in trajectories free of my
will
or influence
into the loneliness
of deep space
and blanket of stars
guidance systems have malfunctioned again
i seek a new north star
holding my breath
hoping for the best
cold numbing my outstretched fingers

a swarm of letters

a swarm of letters
rustles in my head
pulls me up and out
coffee
dogs
kisses
symphony of birds
whistling their hearts out
in choruses that bring harmony to the world
and chaos of stars
hiding just behind the dawn sky
summoning aspirational dreams
into sounds lining up in my head
and soft clicking of the keys
brushing up against your synapses
in an attempt at communication
love
mystery

desire
and the infinite feeling
of
home

oh, right... yoga

i always forget
then i see her again
yoga babe
rising pulse
calm warrior one
hot hot hot
the thing i can't seem to remember
yoga
yes
shavasana and all that
the year it almost saved my marriage
each morning
after the kids were packed off to school
the vhs tape brought us together
balancing and stretching
breathing toward a peaceful moment
together
and alone

with our breathing
"there is no rescue coming," she said

perched

she felt the sadness inside herself
she saw the pain in her husband's eyes
she remained steadfast in her decision
to rescue herself
required massive action
she was brave
she held his hand and told him exactly why
he was enough
but not right for her
she was leaving
and not returning

there were kids to consider
but her survival was even more important
there was money, houses, and schedules
that would all get worked out
but for now
she needed to leave
alone

set sail for what's next
go eat pray and love somewhere
that was not next to her husband

he was still her husband
he expressed his disbelief, then his anger, then his sadness
became quiet
more silent than she had ever seen him
it was as if the fire had gone out inside of him
she couldn't dally
it was time to move along
before the reasons to stay
became clear
"how convenient for you," said the man
many years ago
"that you only study women"

where was she headed?
would love rejoin her
when the time was right
had she BRAVED her last BRAVE?

as she headed for the door
she hesitated for a second
what if her bigger challenge was to stay
what if the stronger act, the braver act
would be to stay
fight, pray, cry, tussle
and see where that took them all

but it was really over this time

her heart yearned for the open road
the lack of commitments and chores
the untethered joy
of nowhere to go
and plenty of time to get there
she stepped into the sunlight
after days of snow, ice, and cold
and the rays on her face kissed her
she knew
i am okay
he is okay
they are all okay

in this life
we are ultimately alone
we long to have a running buddy
pull their train alongside ours
and run side-by-side up into the mountains
of love and the journey of discovering love together
and then one train fails
a split in the track offers divergent paths forward
and she knew this time
it was for her
it was the harder choice
it was the right choice
and alone
she would discover new answers
and edges of her soul
in loneliness
in ecstasy in the wilderness, alone

alone
she walked out of her marriage
and beyond the edge of the unknown
she was brave
she was smiling
she knew this was the moment
for her to explore
vigorously

how to let you go

how long will i look for a face
among the throng
roaming the whole foods beer section
and notice
an absence
missing in action
gone like yesterday
there is no metaphor that fits
and no messages coming back
too busy
chaos
still not one thing i can do about it
keep moving up and away
allow 'if onlys' to recede
and this ache in my chest
to inherit new meaning
no longer missing
but missing

big love
i knew once

brené brown's
divorce

she felt the sadness inside herself
she saw the pain in her husband's eyes
she remained steadfast in her decision
to rescue herself
required massive action
she was brave
she held his hand and told him exactly why
he was enough
but not right for her
she was leaving
and not returning

there were kids to consider
but her survival was even more important
there was money, houses, and schedules
that would all get worked out
but for now

she needed to leave
alone
set sail for what's next
go eat pray and love somewhere
that was not next to her husband

he was still her husband
he expressed his disbelief, then his anger, then his sadness
became quiet
more silent than she had ever seen him
it was as if the fire had gone out inside of him
she couldn't dally
it was time to move along
before the reasons to stay
became clear
"how convenient for you," said the man
many years ago
"that you only study women"

where was she headed?
would love rejoin her
when the time was right
had she braved her last brave?

as she headed for the door
she hesitated for a second
what if her bigger challenge was to stay
what if the stronger act, the braver act
would be to stay
fight pray cry tussle
and see where that took them all

but it was really over this time
her heart yearned for the open road
the lack of commitments and chores
the untethered joy
of nowhere to go
and plenty of time to get there
she stepped into the sunlight
after days of snow, ice, and cold
and the rays on her face kissed her
she knew
i am okay
he is okay
they are all okay

in this life
we are ultimately alone
we long to have a running buddy
pull their train alongside ours
and run side-by-side up into the mountains
of love and the journey of discovering love together
and then one train fails
a split in the track offers divergent paths forward
and she knew this time
it was for her
it was the harder choice
it was the right choice
and alone
she would discover new answers
and edges of her soul

in loneliness
in ecstasy in the wilderness, alone

alone
she walked out of her marriage
and beyond the edge of the unknown
she was brave
she was smiling
she knew this was the moment
for her to explore
vigorously

leaving us

i believe in spirits of the dead
they don't haunt me
but around me they swirl
if I take a moment to say hello
i might get an answer
a warm or cold feeling
as if...
and it's not just my family
my mother and brother
who took their walk
across the rainbow bridge
are around and nodding their heads
it is more about the others
dads of high school buddies
or high school friends
from other high schools
there is something about them
that strikes me differently

their entire untold story
and collapse of my opportunity
to ask them about their memories
of all the wildness we put them through
when we were bent on driving
ourselves down the highway to hell
as fast as our first cars would take us
today is one of those days
lazy summer heat beginning to bloom
into the ides of march
putting a punch in the gut
about the return to offices
and cubicles
and managers with trust issues
i am not all here today
i am chatting with José
seeing his flamboyant and boyish smile
and how i wished for a dad that was involved
today i ask for a blessing
this is it
this moment is the beginning and the end
today is just another turn of el sol
and i am here to celebrate
cry
and remember
promises and hugs
that cannot go with them
where they have gone
and yet
i feel them

the minute i frame a question
"do you talk to her"
this psychic asked about my dead sister
"what do you mean?"
"just, ask her, she will answer."

and that's my spirituality
in a poem
prayer
words on a computer screen
as pink floyd croons on about
"where were you"
and here I am
here i be
all by myself
and surrounded by love

as the night cools

as the night cools
and the lights swirl in the waves
i imagine your voice
telling me something whispering
about spain
about kisses
about a moment only dreamed
a sad piano jingles
rays of dying light merging
blue and orange
and stars that we can't yet see
above people we miss
hearts we'd love to hug again
whoosh whoosh sound of water
as a boat destined for home
slices the glass-like lake
racing into the coming darkness
warmth of the day is done

the grass is cool and damp
under my feet
walking back towards
my solitude
i am amiss
cooler air is pushing day to night
and the dead sleep of the living
well played
ready for reset
on things i didn't get to
lovers i didn't call
and prayers
still spilled
as the night cools

just outside of your
front door

just past the open door
love is blooming
in the seaside pool
bearded bear envelopes
tattooed and tiny
it's a scene
perhaps
more appropriate
in private
yet darling
hopeful
it's 72 degrees
in texas
the sun is bright
the sky is clear
and the waves appear murky

through the gate
and i can hear her laugh
i think i heard her mention
streaming
this afternoon
her work, his work, their work
live streaming
with fewer clothes
taking requests
from their fans
but for a few hours
the pool
the beach
the early afternoon
yeti cooler
full of silver bullets

i can see only one
werewolf

– corpus christi

sex and coffee

it's better than coffee
a bare midriff mid-morning
in my feed
now pulsing through my veins
dopamine you're a wicked mistress
candy or sex or danger
all three
and i'm in heaven
for 45 seconds
when i find myself
wanting more more more
and ten minutes has passed
nothing accomplished off my todo list
nothing but white noise
and the image
how i wanted to be in that bedroom
in black and white
with an amazing reader

who happens to be holding my coffee
"yes, i'll take that please"
all in some random flash
a vixen
might as well be on another planet
at least until the end of the day
when i can ask
for a reenactment with someone
closer to my field of vision
within my reach

just a second

walk outside right now
stop stop stop the rush
of this day and moment
and go breathe a cloud in
take a pause to collect
the pieces of your soul
scattered out along the rush
of this work
this adventure
this life

you know
there is no other chance
this is the big show
you should not be waiting
for some sign
if you are
this poem is the sign you were waiting for
don't wait

go outside
stop driving so hard and fast
open yourself to the softness of an afternoon's heat
to the smell of the cedar
even as it makes your eyes water
give space for god
or your higher power
to catch up with you
don't hurry on
don't interrupt
just listen to a few good deep breaths
IN
and
slowwwwly
OUT
pause
repeat

this break brought to you by war
nearby deaths
tornadoes touching down next door
and all that is sacred in our lives
but ignored
escaped through entertainment
missed with resentments and anger
this break
is the beginning
the opening
for your change to happen

now
right now

in this second
with each word of a poem
you are opening to the pause
the great pause
the slow inhale and exhale
the modern recovery act
i am only here as a friend
a lover
a colleague
in every interaction i hope to encourage
champion
and cheer
for your success
as we both learn to slow it all down
this work/life balance destination
and do it now
do it even if we don't feel it
do it because it will take effect
more powerfully than any antidepressant
more than sex, or chocolate, or money
the pause
the connection with another person
could be the most two vital practices on the earth

with these words, these strokes of keys on a laptop
i am joining with you
calling for your moment of connection

with your inner voice
your breathing
and your tuning in and dropping out
of the furious pace of your world
please pause
please take the breaks you need
please celebrate those around you
at every moment
and know that i am with you
in this journey to aim our hearts
closer to the beloved
i am here
you are there
we
are
in this most sacred
now

woman on cloud

maybe
you are thin
rich
wearing new white on clouds
requesting a large esoteric coffee chai oat milk no foam mix
as your reward for a tough private yoga lesson
you are single
unsure of the meaning of your life
beyond being kind
and beautiful

and if i met you
again for a second or third time
you are a friend's ex-girlfriend
and the first thing you notice
comment to my friend
about
is my weight
as we are heading up to go snow skiing

making a pitstop to drop off the fancy dog
that she still loves
and my friend
also mentions his concern
for my health
as he vapes 30 – 40 times an hour

i'm thinking we have a disconnect
on most levels of existence
still
you are pretty to look at
speeding out the door
cup in hand
blonde hair in a tiny bob
underneath your
resort cap

– santa fe

a word and

my mind travels in bookshops all over the world
searching for the answer
the place for my poetry to find purchase
audience
laughter
and the smell of bookstores
light conversation with cashiers
and their old growling goldens
it's best with a cup of coffee in hand
browsing the staff selections
the section titles
the points of focus for each demographic being served

here
today
new mexico
writers
how to write
southwest fiction

southwest non-fiction
southwest writers
southwest architecture
native/queer authors

each spine calling out
with color
adjectives
letters of promise
and the comfort of more books than i could read
in a lifetime of reading

my mind keeps filling up
with phrases
images
mountain watercolors
stormy skies asking to be captured
on this day of rest
i can smell love poems
and books on how to draw southwest landscapes
it's no wonder i don't want to leave
except to try and tap in
a few letters in sequence
attempting an embrace
of the joy
in
this
~~place~~
moment

sheer pleasure

prancing like gazelles

20-year-old yoginis

leave little to our imagination

more for our proclivity

than theirs

proud and glistening

from downward dogs

and shivasanas

my lunch is less interesting

than the parade

of exclusive brand shoes

and sweatless wonders

of god's creation

she was

the dream i kept building
turning towards the dawning waves of daylight
as if i'd never known

love

the dream i was leaning into
along the rocky shores of courtship
saying the right things
to each other

to keep any dream alive
both lovers must contribute
adoration multiplied
sarcasm assassinated
in one simple action
repeated several times a day

"i can't wait to kiss you"

your brain

twitching inside to understand

just how much your brain

turns me on

lights go on all over my living rooms

when we connect

over poems

writers

love languages

that join in

hyper-connections

even when distant

invisible contacts

transmit small particles

adorations

as we glide along our chosen paths

fluidly alone

drawn toward

one another

as if magnetic

across time

and

space

random access

memories

warm synapses fire
cool bullets of dopamine
at my unfocused morning mind
she is there
always there
a deep dart that cannot be removed
only scraped over
compartmentalized
rebuffed losses
still suspended in ambergris
and sensual chemical codes in my brain
unlocked and loaded
aimless

no return from

murano

getting off the boat on the wrong side of venice
gave my new wife and me
time to explore the alley-side of it all
walking through the tiny open squares
littered with kids, cafe tables, and clinking glasses
she was in a sundress and cold
i was trying to look bigger and meaner than I was
mostly, it was old ladies
peering out of their high windows with a frown
but we never spoke
trying to blend in
lost
and there was something in that moment
a vulnerability i was feeling
about the beautiful woman next to me
and her fear

her silence
hints of the losses to come
on our honeymoon
she became unreachable
as i clung to her hand
pulling us along the dank narrow alleys

she takes her shirt
off

there is a moment
things are not going well
and
she takes her shirt off
it was a ninja move
catching me off guard
unbalancing my argument
with other urges
desires
that required far less discussion

this time
i didn't indulge her
the elephant was making noise
it was time to get clear
about our rapt attention
and sustainability

so
there she was
looking confused
her beautiful naked magic fairy dust move
proved ineffective
this was a deeper conversation

and our last

my girlfriend is

magic

this is not a photo of my girlfriend's fingers and toes
but in this photo is everything i need
coffee
kisses
a hint of sensual exploration as friday begins
now
we are not at the beach, she and me
it's a trick
to find the beach within every weekend
every evening together
every friday night after work
accelerating into the time-of-no-time

in this photo
posted by someone on twitter
i am captivated by the story
words blending in my mind

flooding my normal morning routine
reminding me how lucky we are
to find love in a cup of coffee
in an image from the internet
in the anticipatory joy
of tonight
and tomorrow
and so forth

escape syndrome

out

away

time off

why am i often fantasizing about escape

from a comfortable and nourishing life

job is good

love life is better than ever

house is comfy and full of musical instruments

and still

the ocean

the mountains

the italian mountains that spill over from france

a vespa in florence

kisses on the coast of ibiza

and

here and now

is blurred for a moment

i forget

i long for something i don't have
a new guitar car house pair of tennis shoes
if i listen long enough
maybe i can understand more about my lust
leaving as adventure
muting the demands of this typical life
for a moment in the tuscan sun
or a white churched mountaintop
a tiny cup of bitter coffee standing at the counter
with my lover
always with my lover
i traveled alone in my 20s and 30s
scribbling journals across europe
more longing
ache
ennui
i don't want to say it
loneliness
and perhaps that's the answer
escaping loneliness
is a lifetime goal of mine
and something about traveling with your lover
with no other commitments
provides a freedom
for falling
again and again
in distant cities

blue light

a stream of characters
beamed over the radio waves
to a tower
to a wire
to a data center
to a router
to a wire
to a tower
to your phone

i love you

the ether

silence

are you okay
how are you feeling
what's new
i don't think it's depression

i think it might be the blue light
that keeps me from sleeping
and waiting for my phone
to light up
at any hour
from your response

the sigh of a dog

beside me
the furry beast of desire
sleeps almost immediately
after a huge
sigh

what is it that he's worried about
is it more of a mantra or release
i've been picking up the habit
when changing my mode
inhale
big sigh
let it all go
even this poem

magnetic tagging
of my bloodstream

i'd vape you like pineapple chill if you were here
breathing deep of your spice and sweetness
hold
count to five
dragon fire bursts in white
what is the vapor you have left inside me
how did your scent and smoothness find purchase
in the magnetic tagging of my bloodstream
as i was looking the other way

love poem on

demand

for my birthday she said
i want a love poem
except
the time had passed
we were heading apart
she had limited relationship skills
and zero interest in being friends
with my kids
at first
i was so grateful for the rescue
she had provided
i thought *recovery* would be enough
to hold me fast
keep me optimistic
but the dream
occurred more than once

i was in a high place

clowning around with the edge

until i was falling

with a sense of fear and acceleration

that continued

long after i was awake

navigating

passively hostile waters

from a high hotel room in Spain

with a woman i had grown to blame

for the failure

in the place of loss

and loneliness

i have lived
in the place of loss and loneliness
listened to the song of myself
aching
reaching
toward
some infinite longing unfulfilled
as if
this sadness was my natural state

i have fallen for a girl
taken pains to weave together
beloved after beloved
only to crash into this emptiness again

what is it in my optimistic heart
that continues this quest

how do my arms continue to open
to the threat of love and loss and disappointments

i have no superpower
other than desire
my heart exploding in letters
arranged across a screen or page
into hope
into flames of unrest
and ultimately
into a new set of promises
to have and to hold
to appreciate and adore
to ignite foolishly into dark nights
in the arms of an available lover
somehow able to meet these rigorous demands
of honesty
vulnerability
and mutual aspirations
and the unrelenting "yes"
that can come from holding the hand
of the one
true
love

72

streaming now

i found myself at home

at rest

and excited at the same time

i could not lose

in the arms of love

so i learned to rest

open

breathe and stretch

streaming now

not enough kisses

i already know there is not enough time
to tell you
now that i've found you
how grateful I am
not enough nights
to kiss you
not enough ways to say
i love you
we're already behind
so i will do my best
each day of our time together
to let you know
you are beautiful
important
and loved

74

losing the thread

i keep losing the thread
how we could get closer
follow along the edge of the creek
looking for a shady spot
to rest
cast a fly or two
breathe in the sunshine
and crisp new mexico spring afternoon
but i am in texas
only recalling your hand
the soft sound of your voice
lilting easy laughter

and she was

and she was in front of me
today
like every other day
and today
i stopped
to praise her beauty
i forget sometimes
and her smile
transformed my being
into something more light
her warm embrace
even as I could not see her eyes
summer's warming zepher
as the sweat drips
she is with me
lifting me
from the inside
a mood of unusual size

blowing through my body
as we dance
on the beach
in the snowy woods above Taos
in the warm waters
of Oho Caliente
and she is always here
somedays
i forget to see

change of plans

i wanted her exactly as she appeared
i wanted a change
i asked
i prayed
love languaged
yelled
whispered
kissed
self-loved
inspired
lost
left
returned
left again
broke down
died
reanimated
to let go of

one

more

dear heart

what's taken out

poetry
is not
a craft that is in demand
we still teach it in schools
ask elementary kids to give it a try
with no rhyme or reason
to the usefulness
and no real way to justify
the art of less
as a vocation
you could go into advertising
journalism
and still
parents are amazed
by the scattered words
with a crayon illustration
that captures
love

growth
loss
god, even

what's taken out
is miscellaneous

an aspiration

she is stronger than i know
more beautiful than i've had a chance to discover
reaching for her lover
with grace and a smile
to light 1,001 nights
beyond where i've ever been
and she knows
i am beside her
every step of the way
even as the course corrections may be numerous
this flight plan
is one we've both been drawing on our own
praying for a copilot
for the heavy weather
as well as ice cream sundaes
rainbow fkn unicorns
we are
she is

girl in waves

she said my presence in her life
was no longer a priority
as she left for three weeks in hawaii
i stayed calm
as I stayed in her place
awaiting

her return
did bring a moment
of clarity
as i volunteered to give her more space
it was as if
we had been living to two separate worlds
me still loving as hard as i could manage
her establishing a different plan
that didn't include me

i
showed myself out

still howling at the loss
and dancing alone
in the moonlit waves
closer to home
lone wolf
again

84

the farther i fall

in the blue sky
the hope for a season of love
in the snowy nights
and stormy days
ahead
optimism points to yes
to you
with me

i drink winds

drink winds
like a fabled monster
swallowing the ocean
i become bloated with ideas
dreams
songs
letters that beg
to be turned into a poem
i travel to find new breezes
i ask companions to join me
in the ecstasy
blowing
along
inhaling every second
trigger point
fingertip
tongue
laugh

waves arriving

waves retreating

and the moon

her tides

and mysteries

and blessing

just breathe

winter berries

cold races in
whispers your absence
bed empty and disheveled
pillow tightly held
a wet winter day
beckoning to me
retreat
relapse
rest
release

i want to live

i want to live in the mountains
among the pines and snow
where eagles streak the sky
and white smothers all sound
and despair is blanketed
in god's fairy dust
i can feel the high
in a photo
i can recall the sound of your laugh
your strong pace
and winning leap
into my arms
i hope it is lovely up there
i am not coming soon
but i hold you always
in my heart
as my first

big
love

imagine the ending

flying home
november again
towards myself
limitless
unbound
ready for more
skipping over the painful bits
with abandon
and vigor
this is not the time
for regrets
or fear
or compromise
today
this year
i claim my independence
and self-care
self-love

selfishness
it is only on lonely nights
that i compose
love songs
heartbroken poems
and aspirational lists
of my *next* partner

it always ends like this
alone
logging into bumble
like a boss
opening new horizons
new opportunities
for more
for less
for smashing good sex
and less than joyful
collisions
my degree is in romance
not chemistry
i throw caution to the wind
for a pretty face
a smile that ignites
nightlights in my mind
and flutters in my belly
"she is the one"
i like to write
"she might be the one"
i write after a few months

"she's got issues"
i muse
trying to repair the landing gear
mid-flight
adjusting the airspeed
and frictional drag
as we feel the tips of the trees
frozen and fragile
from the winter freeze
the power outage
that puts a point on everything
we're lacking
that's broken
in our energy grid
in our cooperative contracts
spoken and hidden
i write what i will miss
i write about being alone again
i write
more than i cry
about the loss
of one more missed embrace
moon shot at happiness
more dead roses
and a lifelong romance
imagined and constructed
and negotiated
until the path forward
became overgrown with brambles
and dangerous snares

set out for predators past
and triggered
at odd times
without rhymes
without reasonable doubt
merely set off
severing limbs
setting off alarms
breaking down lines of communication
until an exit
is the natural
result
and this poem
the obvious
motion
of my crushed
optimism

patterns

l e t t

e r

s

patterns
expressing

e

mo

tion

more random

than not

more clear at times

than syntax

overthinking

over

word

ing

this then
is not a love poem
as you might have surmised
but a
pattern of
lines
to
crudely outline

this word
vs
that sound
vs
love
hunger
lust
sadness
etc

another
completed
exercise
aimed at space
launched into this vacuum
via
bits
bytes
and the webby wonder we weave

with the donkeys

no one is here to give directions
we're just livin as best we can
amongst the beggars and thieves
the hookers and politicians
we the walking dead
don't look up from our devices
we don't answer our phones
or text back in a timely manner
even that idea
is
stupid
let's just talk
spend some time together
but...
that's it
right?
that's the issue
time is essential for building relationships

and if you don't have any to give
idgaf
i mean
i do
but
well...
you understand
we're all with the donkeys

boomland

the days of wine and roses were long gone for boomland residents
kmart and sears had both gone bankrupt vacating the mall
a wasteland of modern progress in a small illinois suburb
where my lover escaped my reach and blocked all connections

finding shade

rivers have run dry
temps raise to 110 degrees
where the blacktop will melt sneakers
tires
and bare feet bottoms
since the fuel ran out
travel during the day consists of finding shade
along your walk
if you've got a bike
even better
you can find an oasis of deflection
at longer intervals
if your tires don't explode from the heat

she disappeared

putting herself out of reach
goes with her behaviors in the past
how her schedule
her son's schedule
included "you can come if you'd like"
rather than
"would you like to..."
i was always an afterthought
maybe a red flag
i tried to be flexible
the bigger man
understanding

what i didn't realize
is how my heart was being crushed
i was building a partnership
she was enjoying a helpful man
in a passing moment
time was an issue

time alone was impossible
to say the word enmeshed
would be an understatement

she's retreated back to her college stomping grounds
to find her next move
her son's next adventure
and a winter that will become colder and colder
until her progeny alights for new horizons
she can bide her time and her desires
for eight or so more years
when the decisions
might be more independent
where he thinks for himself
that can only be delayed so long
and then her son
will wound her deeply
simply by being
a man

last poet

had a quiet exit
no media outlet was alerted
cable news had nothing
even reddit was silent
as silent as the poems
not to be written
or read
or spoken to anyone

if you google it
you might find yourself
here
thank you
but this isn't the story

there isn't a story
or a poem
left
to describe

the infinite loss
when a wordcrafter
loses
fire

bird

accelerating into the afternoon
i was surprised
by an invisible barrier
keeping me from my
purpose
nap
food

smack
i woke up on the ground
looking up at the heated texas blue sky
a sizzling sound in my ears
the smell of bar b que
my back on the asphalt of life
roasting
along with the planet

aliens
can't arrive soon enough

coffee could be stronger
like those memories of my youth
driving hard at the goal
the objective, thesis, big harry ass goal

i'm a bit better now
in the shade
contemplating essential moves
fluids
her accidental exit
a future trajectory
and arc of the day

deep learning

over time
i learned that my love
was big
effusive
effervescent
and occasionally too much
even for me

as i've grown
i understand my energy
to be puppy-ish
and some partners want a cat
so even as i'm pouring more into them
they are feeling overwhelmed
confused
like everything is going too fast

a dog in my life today
frodo

has taught me what i look like
to others
he is always there
always willing
first into the bed for a nap
always up for a snack
and looking for reassurance

as i've grown more into a man
i am learning to dial it back
and listen more
pause more
give my partner a moment
and the silence
confidence to breathe easy
and wait

even Frodo leaves the bed
when he's bored or wakeful
he escapes to his red chair
for alone time
and rest
until someone else is awake

"look at this day, dad"
first let me have some coffee

give more than you think possible
and also give space
for the echoes of indecision
of a hand in hand

smiles all around
and the massive joy that comes
feeling
how deeply you are loved

opened books

there are twenty-seven open or bookmarked books in this
house
right now
i counted them
a bit like my mind
my creative ideas
rush in grabbing time and sparks of ignition
and then another one
i have to bookmark or pause
and try to root out the magic of the next
idea
like this one
take a photo
write something and

fires from long ago

hard to remember
the hurts and fires
started by your ex
looking through the snowy dawn
the glow
is the love of god
for all the arrows
you left in the quiver

tuckered out

and just then
the moon
in the morning sky
woke something sad inside me
like holden
watching phoebe on the carousel
in the last pages
the poetry of sallinger
and
the morning
and
the dogs waking up
sounds of their flap
in and out
their paws making a crunch sound
on the crispy brown grass

this summer of joy
endless

as my hand on your back
the nape of your neck
3 am
and
warm smiles
i feel from here
beside the plunge pool
a moment

the most beautiful

girl is okay

holding a big gulp(tm) outside the mcdonald's
and waiting for me
or someone
for a ride
she's fit
her headscarf wrapped tightly over her dark luxurious curls
falling down her back
she's tan
smiling
it's 104 degrees in the shade
and she's not eaten for a day and a half
if nobody notices
she can refill her cup
with carbonated sugar water
but she could really use a big mac(tm)
or a boyfriend

or a friend
a campsite nearby has lots of men
no safe ones
i can still see the smirk in her eyes
as she assesses the likelihood of my support
and moves on toward the back of the parking lot
through a gap in the fence
and gone
a mirage of her once-glorious
days
before the planet was on fire
and summers were about getting high and laid

slip sliding away

there is danger and sadness inside me
a dance that i no longer recognize
with a partner who pushes
when pulling would be the gift
dazzling skyline calling for adventure
entertainment
dancing

...

i can't speak about it too much
the wounded bear is still hanging around
giving bad advice
poking my soft places
for a reaction
a response
an answer
to the
misstep
i still struggle to understand

on the wire

again

no longer a seeker

of love

i am no longer a seeker of love
it has arrived
stripped me naked
howled
cried
laughed

i cannot see god but through love
and i am
fully empowered
enlightened
humbled
by another heart

as big as mine
and different
able to contain my sorrows

hold my regrets
celebrate my little victories
pause in the silence
of the unknown

together
provides exponential opportunities
and challenges
as the unknown
edges closer
and my fears and hopes
co-mingle in soft resting places
and the cradle of her arms

none of us can see into the future
but we hope for the best
lean into the other person
for absolutely everything
leaving no objection unvoiced
no passion unstoked
no future impossible

here i will find salvation
for a moment
of celebration and prayer
as we dance
alongside each other
like trains
aligning
in some distant
desert city

a cold midnight
and the sound of rusty metal
pushing and pulling
burnishing bright
the harsh edges
of the frigid night
and long journey ahead

i am no longer a seeker of love

my love

is beside me

mecca

i used to sit here
trolling for beauty
and fresh mint
a coconut coffee creamer
and a lover

today
i find
the youth and beauty overrated
the produce dull
and the longing for love
an absent
ghost

the vapors
no longer skew my view
longing lust loss
hunger

nothing is missing in my life
at this moment

amen

in this moment
i am loved
at peace

stripping down to null

pulling the fine threads of affection out of the heart
is a delicate procedure
gone from my eyes and my arms
still the ache the loss the longing
lingers like a cruel flu
haunting plans for escape
moments of levity
release
love removal
recalibration
a power wash
steam clean the chambers
both blue and red
inhale and exhale
with words of comfort
in with the good the pure the spiritual light

out with all memories
kisses
moments of one
moments of never again
moments lost
not yet excised by time or breath or prayer
serenity is part of a process now
a releasing of expectations
learning
that i am the issue
my heart is the source of the pain
my longing
an emptiness
no amount of food or drink can fill
nor time remove
without the painful scrubbing
beneath the paint and the skin
blinks of blissful connection
now gone dead
forever
removed

in time

ping

in the waving of the golden leaves
i notice the chill
the sound of rustling
and a shrill "ping"

my ears search for the source
piercing my reverie
smoke from backyard projects
brings me back to the moment
light dancing golden with promise
"ping"

a neighbor has a new car
a new alarm system
saying "ready"
"ping"

we're being swallowed by ai
they say

and tech we can't control
or understand
sort of like love
or longing for love
on a november dawn
"ping"

crap
all poetry is useless
ai writes good limericks
by arranging letters and words
into the next best word sentence paragraph
"ping"

in a mimic of language
copy paste of a billion ideas
blended and blurred into form
as useless as trying to meow to your cat
the cat appreciates the effort
"ping"

no soul in the machine
anti poet society
hyper-sales entertainment
and pharma miracles to make you happy
thin
loved
"ping"

i spent a summer in the mountains
aspen leaves laughing at my breathing

napping
longing
hope
and

zero ping

rip-roaring fury of

fun

let's say you're in a starbucks somewhere
for the wifi and coffee cake
listening to music
admiring the crowd waiting for their boosts
and trying to form letters and words
while keeping an eye on the bathroom line
"i've got to make it through, no matter what it takes"
mixing and melding
thoughts words sounds and ideas
for some coherent grasp
at meaning
love
contentment
in the city that never sleeps
all getting jacked on exotic blends
late afternoon lull

interrupted by a rush

cold or hot

no care

of sleep

ever

go go go

push push

productivity or death

rip it

roar it

burn brightly

until

…

– nyc

missing

i was looking from here
from where i exist
and noticed something missing
or gone

you

15 seconds of life

the site was taking a long time to load
i had to pee
my phone was on 3%
and my coffee was making me jittery
i needed food
bandwidth
and quiet beyond what my noise-canceling buds provided

a burst of words
poetry
at each pause
stuck in traffic = poem
hold music = poem
slow internet
you get the idea

what is 15 seconds worth
inertia
stop

pause
breathe
mad mad madness

black friday came and went without notice
the sale will continue through infinity
and the hollow feeling
creeping in
won't vape away
it is a question
an xiety
what has gotten you down
impatience all around
even inside
word searching for a closing
bat
shit
crazy

blip – gotta go – see ya

any and all

impulses must be examined
rejected
delegated
stored
or acted upon immediately
like sparks blowing into the sky
on a cold winter evening
in las vegas
new mexico
with two friends
talking quietly about the stars
the journey ahead
and love
mostly loss
mostly dark spots of pain
lingering
long after the flight has been tamed
and fight

restrained
and this moment
this very moment
if we can listen
capture
love wide and hard
can become a bright memory
to examine
in time
as a high note
in a symphony of sorrow
loss
economic and spiritual collapse
i reach back to you
no longer seeking comfort
or interactions
with others
me
in hopes
a reawakening of energy
is forthcoming
warm
and
full of lazy afternoon naps
entwined like vines
loneliness
just out of frame
hearts feel the danger
before our minds
can adjust

our narrative

and

it

is

gone

violà

how come viola is not pronounced with a vee
and cello has a che sound instead of a cee
i wonder at the words racing in me
at the speed of light
or loss
somewhat determined by my caffeine intake
a virus of the mind
i think
i have
you have it to
i simply choose to listen closely
and release bits and bytes
into the ether
of nominal value
to others

exit stage left (last flight of "the rocket")

full of myself
mindful enough
merely a player off stage today
the last titan in my life
the rocket
left a week ago
destination unknown
loss of signal
in a series of endings
reorienting
all i hold dear
actions
input v output
pause + quiet

moments captured in amber
frankincense pungent and true
provide a focus
for
thoughts tumbling
through

– for rdk sr.

word by word

like the dreary mist falling
poems
announce themselves
at inopportune moments
either
pause and capture

or

release

back to the
void

i was going to wear a suit
the best i could manage
were black jeans
cowboy boots
and a bit of extra
jiz in my hair

singing
celebrating the last rocketeer
in an ever-ascending burn

receptive

in moments of life
we experience pockets of great change
listen
learn
be fucking quiet for a change
just

pause

i know it's hard
out of character
and the great lesson of your life
don't strike out for the shore
until you know where you want to be

word here
cup of coffee
misty morning

optimism
hope

if
i
can
slow my roll

right
fucking
no

w